Teaching the Craft of Writing

Organization

by Lola M. Schaefer

New York • Toronto • London • Auckland • Sydney
Mexico City • New Delhi • Hong Kong • Buenos Aires

Dedication

For young writers everywhere

Acknowledgments

I appreciate these teachers who shared their insights as well as samples of student work:

* Marolyn Krauss at Horizon Elementary School

* Michele LaFever and Carolyn Fletcher at South Adams Elementary School

* Jaime Brunson at J. E. Ober Elementary School

* Darla Kingrey and Ann Hollar at Horace Mann Elementary School

Thank you to my editors, Joanna and Sarah, who both continue to be a source of inspiration and support.

And, I offer my sincere gratitude to student writers, who willingly experiment and tell us what works best for them.

* * *

Cover Design by Maria Lilja
Cover Illustration by Kristen Balouch
Interior Design by Sarah Morrow

Copyright © 2006 by Lola M. Schaefer
All rights reserved.
Published by Scholastic Inc.
Printed in the U.S.A.
ISBN 0-439-44400-4

1 2 3 4 5 6 7 8 9 10 40 11 10 09 08 07 06

Table of Contents

Introduction 4

Chapter 1 ✳ What is Organization?:
Introducing Organization to Students 5

Chapter 2 ✳ Student Writers and Organization:
Helping Students Develop Organization 11

Chapter 3 ✳ Organizing for Personal Narrative 16

Chapter 4 ✳ Organizing for Story 27

Chapter 5 ✳ Organizing for Poetry 37

Chapter 6 ✳ Organizing for Information Writing 42

Bibliography 47

Introduction

For the past eight years, I have been a visiting writing coach in elementary and middle schools. During my residencies, the students and I create our own original pieces of writing from an initial idea through revision. During this three- to five-day writing process, we are constantly working on craft. Craft is the art of using tools and skills to produce meaningful text.

As I work with student writers, I envision that each of them has a writing backpack. Our job as teachers is to provide students with strategies that become life-long tools they can carry with them in these backpacks. How do we do this? We first create a non-threatening writing community where teacher and students experiment with words, side by side. Next, we offer students a rich environment of published literature, modeling, demonstration, practice (lots of practice), and a receptive audience.

What is so encouraging is that I watch student writers embrace these strategies and quickly improve in the craft of writing. Since writing is a form of self-expression, it only makes sense that they would want to know how to do the following:

- use and maintain a writer's notebook
- select and refine an idea
- organize for different purposes and genres
- add interest and information through elaboration
- develop a genuine writer's voice
- write strong leads that lure readers into the text
- create endings that satisfy readers
- revise the piece until it reflects their intent

I believe that students' attention and commitment are strong because they are practicing craft in the context of their own authentic work. Involvement is always more active when writers are able to self-select their topics. They have something to say that is important to them—something they believe and care about. The writing has a purpose and the strategies hold promise to help students realize that purpose.

Teaching craft is more a journey of discovery rather than a precise, step-by-step program. Student writers need to be immersed in a constant study of how other authors craft their work. They need to study published writing such as poetry, story, nonfiction, and memoir. They need well-focused mini-lessons that act as constant reminders of what craft is and what it can do. They need time to reflect, plan, draft, rethink, draft again, revise, and share.

Most important, our student writers need encouragement and support. Celebrate everything they write well. Then, watch your students express themselves in ways you never thought possible.

Chapter 1

What Is Organization?

Introducing Organization to Students

Organization is the act of placing parts in an order, creating structure out of an otherwise random or confused state. It has always been the fundamental building block of good writing. Plato, Shakespeare, Charles Dickens, Abraham Lincoln, E. B. White, and Virginia Hamilton all understood the need for organization in their essays, plays, novels, speeches, and stories. Without organization, an audience has to struggle to make sense of the writing.

Today, organization is always one of the criteria on writing rubrics, and understandably so. It is this element of craft that helps the writer and the reader plot their course through the text. It provides logical progression from one thought to another, giving the reader a level of comfort and familiarity that enables him or her to relax and engage with the meaning of the text.

Since our main goal as teachers of student writers is to offer tools that will help them become independent thinkers and writers, we need to model and teach different ways of organizing writing. This will further students' craft, which in turn will provide a better understanding of how to express themselves. From my experience with students in grades 2–4, I know they are both capable of and willing to learn about external and internal organization.

External Organization

Some people cannot begin to bake until their kitchens are clean and orderly. Others cannot begin to tune up their vehicles until their garages are neat and tidy. Many writers, including me, cannot tackle a large writing project until their books have been re-shelved and their piles of notes have been sorted, filed, or disposed of. I need external organization in my workplace before I can internally organize my thoughts for writing.

Our students have the same requirements. They need an organized setting in which they are able to relax and concentrate. Regie Routman addresses this straight on in her book, *Conversations*. She writes: "I believe it is absolutely essential to have in place an organization system that is easily manageable by the students and teacher. This includes a predictable daily time and space for writing and conferencing, established routines that students and teachers agree on, and systems for storage of writing and record keeping."

No two writing classrooms operate quite the same. However, all efficient and comfortable writing environments need to devote attention to these elements of external organization:

- a designated time in the daily schedule for writing
- regular mini-lessons
- a generous chunk of time devoted to independent work in writing workshops
- a copy of the writing process on display in the classroom
- student writers' notebooks
- storage space for writing folders
- a designated classroom area for peer conferencing
- a specific space for teacher conferencing
- routines for various engagements of the writing process

Classroom Setting

Like a baker's kitchen or a mechanic's garage, student writers require a classroom that is orderly. Routines for the writing workshop need to be established. It takes planning and decision-making on both the teacher's and students' parts to envision how the writers' classroom will be designed and managed. For instance, questions such these need to be addressed:

- *How and where will students record their writing ideas?*
- *How and where will they conference with the teacher?*
- *How and where will students meet with their peers?*
- *What kinds of responses do student authors hope to receive from their peers?*
- *Where can students find references for revision strategies?*
- *How will they decide how often and which pieces to publish?*
- *What type of proofreading and editing is expected in published works?*
- *Will writing portfolios be part of the classroom structure, and where will they be stored?*
- *How often do students need to select pieces for their portfolios?*
- *How will the teacher know where each student is in the writing process on any given day?*
- *When and how often will students read their published works to one another?*

Of all the classrooms I visit, I find that students understand and follow the procedures for writing workshop best when they have been part of the decision-making process from the beginning. Of course, at the start of the year, the teacher needs to thoroughly introduce each engagement and expectation of the writer's workshop to the students. As your students become active participants in all aspects of the workshop, set aside a few minutes each week to define routines. Decide what works best with this group of students. A writing workshop develops day by day, and it matures a little differently with each group. Because of this design, it makes sense to consult with them whenever it's time to make a workshop decision. What's always a little surprising to me is that the students are specific and articulate on how to improve the established routines—but, of course, they know exactly what is working for them and what needs to be "tweaked." In the following paragraphs, I share some examples of my students' input.

In the past, many of my classes have requested that a certain amount of workshop time be designated as "No talk, no walk." These students explained that for their

Taking the Journey Together

As I began my own personal journey into writing for publication, which coincidentally was my first year of classroom teaching, I attended many writers' conferences. I would return to my classroom excited to share my new insights with my students. As I described specific strategies, I would often read passages from the professional books that I had purchased at the conferences. My students listened intently. Afterward, we were all engaged in healthy discussions as we decided what our next steps could be.

The students never considered this advice for adult writers beyond them or out of their reach. We were a community of writers hungry to learn more about our craft.

I never forgot that first year and my students' reactions to the readings. Each year thereafter, I chose passages, sometimes whole books, on the craft of writing to read to my students. Their engagement and enthusiasm never wavered.

Try it! Read portions from your favorite professional books on writing. Ask your students to respond. Establish a dialogue about what works and what you'd like to try next.

The following books can provide you and your students with some solid material on writing workshops and the craft of writing.

- *Conversations: Strategies for Teaching, Learning, and Evaluating* by Regie Routman
- *Live Writing: Breathing Life into Your Words* by Ralph Fletcher
- *Scaffolding Young Writers: A Writers' Workshop Approach* by Linda J. Dorn and Carla Soffos
- *What You Know By Heart: Developing Curriculum for Your Writing Workshop* by Katie Wood Ray
- *Wondrous Words: Writers and Writing in the Elementary Classroom* by Katie Wood Ray
- *Writing Workshop: The Essential Guide* by Ralph Fletcher and JoAnn Portalupi

concentration they needed to have a quiet setting void of distractions and interruptions. For some classes, it began as twenty minutes of our daily writing time. Often that evolved into forty minutes a day. Students almost always suggested that the "No talk, no walk" portion be at least one-half to two-thirds of the entire workshop time. All students respected this quiet time because it was their decision, not something that I mandated.

Over the years, some of my students have wanted to use writing records or logs—a written record of every piece each student has written. They enjoyed looking back and noting the different genres they had written, both independently and as a class. Other classes wanted no part of that. They preferred investing that kind of time in writing responses to peer pieces. Instead of just offering celebrations and helpful nudges aloud at the time of the reading, students would go back to their desks and write detailed notes to the writer. Later, the writer would have several handwritten responses to read over and over again. (And they did!)

Some classes created a routine for how often and what pieces to add to their writing portfolios. They produced a "history" of each piece that included the plan, focus, choice of audience, first draft, revision, final draft, and copy of the rubrics used for evaluation. Students thought this routine would give their parents and them a wonderful overview of the process that led to the final piece. They were right.

As the need for more organization arises during the year, ask your students for advice. However, don't be surprised if they want to revise some of the procedures as the year progresses. As maturing writers, their needs will change. Pull your students together at least once a month, and ask them what is working and what needs to be modified during their writing workshop. They'll surprise you with their insightful recommendations. The more ownership we can offer them, the greater their commitment to their writing.

Classroom Materials: Dictionaries

Writers are wordsmiths. Therefore, students need one of the best tools that can lead them into the world of words—a dictionary.

One of my strongest beliefs about dictionaries is that you only need a few but that each one must be different from the others. For instance, a third-grade classroom might have a picture dictionary, science dictionaries, a large unabridged dictionary, an international dictionary, and pocket and rhyming dictionaries, to name a few. The key is to keep two or three dictionaries out and open at all times. They should be inviting so students want to browse through them.

Individual Materials: Notebooks

From my personal experiences in grades 2–4, I believe that every student writer needs at least two separate spiral notebooks. The smaller of the two can be used as a writer's notebook to record ideas for personal narrative, poetry, story, informational, and letter writing, as well as for words students love, unique pieces of conversation, possible titles, sketches and drawings—all the emotional bits of life that nurture their writing.

The larger notebook can be the place where students plan and draft their pieces. Sometimes, I also have students use the back section of this notebook to take notes on mini-lessons, revision strategies, and editing rules. Many classroom teachers call this "the writing workshop book."

The handiness of keeping all their ideas, plans, and drafts in spiral notebooks is that students always know exactly where to find their works in progress. They are learning one of the good habits of a writer—that each tool has its own place and purpose.

Internal Organization

As teachers, we take internal organization for granted. How could we ever do our jobs if we didn't have a framework for the day, the week, and the semester in our minds long before the morning bell rings? We have mentally filed what we know about our students, the curriculum, human behavior, brain research, learning styles, state and national standards, and different teaching approaches. It's there, in our minds, just waiting to be utilized.

Just as writers need to be organized in their workplaces, they also need to be organized in their minds. Of course, not every writer organizes in the same way. Some authors of fiction explain that they "live" with their characters a long time before they ever put words to paper. Other published writers reveal that they

Mapping My Course

Larry Dane Brimner is the author of more than seventy books of fiction and nonfiction for children. He explains the role organization plays in his process:

One spark often leads to a blaze. I marvel at those writers who say they begin their writing projects with nothing more than a sentence (the spark) and many weeks later have a completed manuscript (the blaze). For me, a story—whether fiction or nonfiction—takes organization. I spend weeks thinking about a book before I commit one word to paper (or disk). I need not only that first sentence, but also an idea of where I'm destined in order to fill in the middle. Organization is the map, if you will, of where I think my characters are going. Of course, my map reading skills are nothing to brag about, and so my characters usually end up taking detours and scenic side-trips on their way toward the destination, which may or may not be that place I thought they were journeying to in the beginning. But the map is the plan that gets them started, and it's perfectly fine if, mid-course, they decide to strike out in a different direction.

You and your class can visit Mr. Brimner's Web site at this address: www.brimner.com.

I don't need to refer to BME in my plans. I already know that from all of my reading. — 4th grader need to create detailed outlines for each and every chapter before they write. Most writers fall somewhere in the middle. They let their ideas brew for many days or weeks. Before they begin writing, they sketch out a general map or plan of how they'd like their writing to develop. Does all writing stay true to the map or plan? Of course not, but having some general sense of where the writing is going helps the author relax. After all, if a writer has a plan, he or she can get serious about language, information, or the emotional events that will take the reader on the intended journey.

> When I plan I try to think of 2–3 things to put in my beginning, then 3–5 things in my middle, and 1–2 things for the ending.
>
> — 2nd grader

Student writers are no different than published writers like Larry Dane Brimner. They, too, need some sort of map or plan before they write. They need to have internal organization before putting pencil to paper. This can sometimes be a daunting job. Not all students come to school prepared and mentally organized. Just take a look inside their book bags or desks to see what I mean. But I know from experience that we can help students learn how to organize their workplaces, materials, and thoughts.

Chapter 1 Review

- Organization is the fundamental building block of good writing.
- Organization offers students a mental framework for their work.
- Students need external organization: the routines and materials of the writing workshop.
- Students benefit from having two notebooks: a writer's notebook to record their own writing ideas, plus the emotional bits of life that contribute to their writing, and a writing workshop book to draft and revise work.

Chapter 2

Student Writers and Organization

Helping Students Develop Organization

The purpose for planning before writing is that the author thinks about the piece. A writer needs to know what the whole will be. When a writer plans, he or she:

- sits quietly and thinks
- concentrates on the piece
- selects an audience and purpose
- discovers the focus of the piece
- decides on the form of writing
- chooses what parts to write and in what order

In other words, when a writer plans, he or she does the hard part up front. I always tell students that writing is ninety percent thinking. If an author thinks long and hard beforehand, the act of writing becomes so much more enjoyable. The greatest benefit from planning is that the author doesn't have to make so many decisions simultaneously. If a writer doesn't plan, then while drafting he must consider audience, purpose, focus, format, organization, and the language he wants to use to convey the meaning of the piece. Any writer can get overwhelmed and derailed while trying to remember all of that. It can also make the actual writing a chore or an unpleasant task. We want to provide planning tools to students so they can break down the writing process into manageable engagements that are rewarding and successful.

Map the Journey

Children have been reading and enjoying Cam Jansen mysteries for more than twenty years. The author of these well-loved stories, David A. Adler, also writes biographies, plus many other books of fiction and nonfiction. He describes organization like this:

> *A story is a voyage with the writer as guide. If our stories, nonfiction too, are aimless, have no real sense of purpose or direction, we'll lose our readers. Organization is the key. An outline is a map for the journey.*

To learn more about Mr. Adler and his books, visit one or both of these Web sites: www.DavidAAdler.com or www.CamJansen.com.

Organize and Then Write

For many years in the classroom, I didn't help my student writers plan before they wrote. I never even thought of it. We would discuss possible writing ideas, read many examples from literature, and then write. I wrote while my students wrote—not in front of them but at my desk. And guess what?! There I was, with more than twenty years of literacy in my hip pocket, struggling to focus and write a fluent piece with organization. (I'm ashamed to admit that back then I never stood in front of my students and modeled. I didn't know what a powerful tool I was denying them.)

The more writers' conferences I attended, the more I heard how beginnings and endings tie together, how you can never really write the beginning of a piece until you know how it's going to end. I also heard more and more about the craft of writing: how to write strong leads, how to use specific vocabulary that provides detail, how to paint pictures with words you choose, and how to write endings that leave your reader satisfied. But I found it difficult to remember all of this and get the piece written at the same time.

Many times I'd have a great idea for a story. I would do just fine with the beginning and part of the middle, but about halfway through my first draft, I wouldn't know where I wanted the story to go, let alone know how it would end. Good story ideas seemed to become fragmented and dissolve right in front of my eyes. Ironically, I noticed my students having the very same problems in their writing.

As I read more professional books and discussed writing with colleagues, I learned that most writers have plans. Some writers of nonfiction labor over detailed plans that resemble outlines. Sometimes, poets begin with a web and later draft a list of words down the page. A few novelists write notes for scenes on index cards and arrange them on the

A Unified Whole

Caroline Arnold is the author of more than 100 books for children on topics ranging from animals and the environment to fossils and ancient cultures. She collects pages and pages of information during her research. Here Arnold explains why she organizes before she writes her books.

When I was a child, my favorite lunch was Campbell's alphabet soup. I loved to fish out the noodle letters and arrange them on my plate until they spelled a word. Writing a book is a little bit like that. I take a jumble of facts and put them together so they make sense. In my book Lion, *I followed two lion cubs through a year of their life. In* Australian Animals, *I grouped the animals by the places where they live. In* Birds: Nature's Magnificent Flying Machines, *I showed how each part of a bird's body helps it to fly. Each book is organized in a logical order to make a unified whole.*

If you and your students would like to read more about Caroline Arnold and her books, visit her Web site at http://www.geocities.com/Athens/1264/.

floor to see the progression of chapters. Some picture book writers dash off a few notes (no real sentences) that show character, problem, plot, and resolution.

So, I tried making a plan myself. Immediately, I realized that once I had a plan, the writing became more enjoyable. My simple plan reflected that organization. I was no longer struggling with making decisions about what would happen next. Instead, I could concentrate on scenes and language. I believe the quality of my first drafts improved as well. Because I did have the freedom to focus on my topic, language, and form, I was able to go deeper into my piece. I could hardly wait to share this insight with my students.

But I needed to be careful. I remembered only too well those detailed outlines that preceded research reports I had to write in grades 4–12. I could see the Roman numerals for the main topics and the lower case letters for the subtopics running down the page. By the time I had read the material and created the two-page outline, I had no desire to write the report. I certainly didn't want to do that to my students. So, I started with simple plans—no more than a few notes. It resembled a skeleton of what I wanted to write. And, at all costs, I tried to avoid the use of complete sentences. I wanted to create an organizational tool that would support student writers, not overwhelm them.

> To plan, I jot down ideas in my yellow note pad.
>
> — 4th grader

Teaching Students About Plans

There are four requirements for a writer before she makes a plan. She must have an important writing idea and know her intentions for audience, purpose, and form. Of course, these variables may change along the way, but it helps to establish them first. When an author is excited about an idea, the enthusiasm helps carry her through the thinking and writing of the piece. When an author knows audience, purpose, and form, it's easier to make decisions about organization, word choice, and sentence structure.

Plans are brief. They need only be a framework or map to guide the first draft. I have two suggestions to prevent a plan from looking like or becoming a first draft. First, ask your students to use only one or two words per note and never complete sentences on their plans. There are several purposes for doing this. I want students to enjoy drawing up their plans and to write just the essentials. Also, every time a writer takes ideas from one context to another, this provides an additional opportunity to reorganize and refine the information. If we want student writers to be thoughtfully engaged in their work, it's helpful to have them progress from a generous supply of ideas in their heads to a few words on paper to detailed writing. Second, ask your students to keep their plans orderly and to skip lines between the different notes. If we expect a plan to be a reference tool, and we certainly will when it's time to write a first draft, then students must be able to navigate and read their plans easily.

Demonstrating Plans to Students

You can introduce plans in two different approaches. One way is to design a series of mini-lessons around plans. With each demonstration, you show a way to create a plan for a different form of writing. Using this approach, the flow of your writer's workshop is not interrupted since students are all selecting different genres to express themselves and using plans that fit their needs. One student may use webs to write poetry. Another student may use a linear plan to design a work of nonfiction. Someone else may use a

Student Writers' Reactions to Plans

I know that student writers I meet like to write. They are anxious to share the emotional events of their lives, to explain their tricky soccer plays or to inform you of the habits of bald eagles. When I give these student writers a choice of topics, they are committed to writing with meaning, focus, strong word choice, and specific details. And if that end takes two or more revisions, so be it. They are willing to invest the time and energy to improve the quality of their pieces.

I know, too, that student writers become more critical readers. The more they write, the more they read and notice how published authors write. Independently, they will go back and reread published materials to see how a certain writer writes his or her leads or how another author shows emotion instead of telling about it. And, as young writers study their craft, they discuss writing with new insight and resolve.

And I know that student writers are eager for instruction and advice. They sit quietly as I plan and write on the overhead projector. They enjoy listening as I make decisions that will impact my writing, sometimes offering their advice whether I request it or not. For example, my student writers absolutely love to help me evaluate my leads. They tell me which ones pull them deeper into the writing and which ones are boring or lack specific detail.

Students quickly learn that different genres dictate their own unique plans when I demonstrate this to them. Soon, they have a backpack of different tools for different jobs. How do my students really feel about making plans before they write? Here's what some of them have told me:

"Once I have a good plan, the writing is easy."

"Making the plan is the hardest work. After that, the writing comes quickly."

"Plans help me think of details that make my writing interesting."

"After you make a few plans, it goes much faster."

"I use different kinds of plans for different kinds of writing."

When I speak with students in grades K–8 about plans, they tell me what works for them and what doesn't. These young writers have helped me formulate my beliefs about the strength and use of a plan for organizing writing. Without their input, I'd still be wondering: *Does a plan really help student writers?*

BME (Beginning, Middle, Ending) plan to write a story. This approach can work quite well. Of course, these mini-lessons need to be repeated throughout the year so students continue to add new plans to their repertoires and explore other genres.

I prefer to use a different approach. I teach the use of plans during two or three weeks of guided writing. By guided writing, I mean a time when the students and I study one genre of writing in detail together. We read several examples of the form we're going to write. Then, I model each step of the different planning processes on the overhead projector while students create their own original plans at their desks. At first, I'm not even asking them to develop their plans into completed pieces of writing. I want them to see the different ways to organize one genre. For instance, I may demonstrate how to plan story with a BME structure. Or I may demonstrate how to plan story with a character, problem, setting, plot, and resolution structure. After the students and I create three to five plans, I ask them to select their favorite story plan and write. In this way, student writers learn strategies to plan one particular genre in a highly supportive environment.

Introduce the planning stages of writing in a way that matches the needs of your students and your own particular teaching style. Let students know that writing takes time and thought. If you model planning for them, they will know that you value this reflective engagement. The more time and effort we spend on thinking before writing, the greater our message to students: Writing is not an assignment; it is a thoughtful tool for self-expression.

The next chapters illustrate how to introduce plans to use with the genres of personal narrative, story, poetry, and information writing.

> *I plan as I go. I think, write, then reread. I do that over and over again.*
>
> — 2nd grader

Chapter 2 Review

- Planning gives an author the opportunity to think and organize before writing.
- Different writers plan in different ways.
- To plan, a writer needs an important writing idea. He or she also needs to identify audience, purpose, and form.
- Plans are brief: they can be a simple framework or a map for the first draft.
- Different genres dictate their own unique plans.
- Plans can be taught in the context of writing workshop or during guided writing.
- Student writers are positive about using plans.

Chapter 3

Organizing for Personal Narrative

At the beginning of the school year, I'm asked into classrooms to help students write personal narratives. It's the natural place to start. Writing about our own emotional events provides a wonderful source of writing ideas. Plus, sharing these highly personal moments helps form a community of writers who know and care about one another.

Mini-Lesson: Modeling and Teaching a Plan

At the beginning of the year I stop often to circulate around the room and make sure everyone is thinking and planning. With students in grades 2–4, I like to repeat this procedure every time I demonstrate a new kind of plan to the whole class. The following mini-lesson shows how I introduce the planning process in the classroom. The plan featured is one of the simplest and provides students with an essential tool.

Mrs. S.: What do writers do?

Tyler: They write things.

Hannah: They write books and stuff like that.

Roy: They sit at home and type on their computers.

Matt: Writers write stories and poems.

Mrs. S.: Everything you said is correct. However, long before a writer writes, he thinks. Thinking is a big part of writing. If a writer thinks about what he wants to write before he begins, his writing is usually much stronger than if he just picks up a pencil and starts putting words on paper. Today we're going to think—long and hard—before we write. As we think, we're going to take notes—short notes. I don't want my hand, or your hands, to get all tired out, so we're only going to write the words we need. We won't write sentences. These notes will make a plan that will help us remember everything we want to write.

Has anyone here ever started writing, and after a few minutes, you couldn't quite remember what it was you wanted to say? I've done that. I've started out all fired up with many good ideas and, pretty soon, I felt as if I were wandering around lost in a field of tall corn. I didn't know what to write next, and I didn't have any idea how to move toward an ending.

I usually get many nods from students at this point, and several hands go up. They can't wait to share their personal frustrations during such moments. This kind of interaction is important. We're talking writer to writer. Students are hearing that not everything I write comes out perfectly the first time. It's reassuring to know that all writers go through some of the same struggles.

Mrs. S.: Can everyone reflect for a moment and decide what you would like to write about today? I've been looking through my notebook, and I've narrowed my ideas to two. I could write about the evening I danced with Santa when I was nine years old. Or I could write about the first time I rode my bicycle to Shoaff Park all by myself. They were both exciting events for me. (*I pause and think for a few moments.*) I've decided to write about my first bicycle ride alone to the park. My audience will be anyone who loves to ride a bicycle, young or old. And my purpose in writing is to share an exciting memory from my childhood. Since we're writing personal narrative this week, that's the form I'll use. Now, I'd like all of you to take a moment and find an exciting, surprising, sad, joyful, or scary memory that you'd like to write about. When you have your writing idea, please look up and smile. (*I wait until I see most of the students are looking at me, smiling.*)

Mrs. S.: Can I hear a few of your writing ideas?

Maya: I'm going to write about riding a rollercoaster for the first time.

Hannah: I want to write about how I got lost in the House of Mirrors at the fair.

Theo: I remember when my sister asked me to go to the scary movie with her.

Tyler: I'm going to write about the day my cat had kittens.

Jana: My Uncle Ray took me fishing and I caught the biggest northern pike.

By now, all of the students seem to be ready with ideas, but I always have several share just in case others need that catalyst of knowing what others are going to write about.

Mrs. S.: Now, I'd like all of you to take a piece of paper and write the word *Who* at the top like this.

I place a transparency on the overhead projector. I write the word *Who* at the top of the sheet. (See page 21 for the completed plan.) Remember to always speak your thoughts out loud as you plan in front of students.

Mrs. S.: I'm going to write about just me because no one was with me on my first bike ride to the park. So, I'll write the word *I* after *Who*.

If you're writing about Uncle Ray and yourself, then put *Uncle Ray* and *I* after *Who*. If you're writing about your cat Muffin, please write *Muffin* and *I* after *Who*. If you were in the House of Mirrors with your cousins, write *my cousins and I*. We know that this piece will be about you. You have to decide if someone else will be mentioned, too. I'll wait while everyone writes something after the word *Who*. Please, do not write sentences like *This is about Mom and me*. Simply write the words *Mom and I* after the word *Who*.

At this time, I take several minutes to travel quickly around the room, making sure everyone is on target.

Mrs. S.: Before we go on, I'd like to hear some of your plans. *(I ask two to four students to share what they've written.)*

Mrs. S.: Who would like to share their *Who*?

Claire: Jerod and I.

Jordan: My aunt Elaine and I.

Nick: My dog Sassy and I.

Mrs. S.: Now, I'd like everyone to write the word *What* beneath the word *Who*.

After the word *What*, I'm going to write the words *bike ride* because that's what I'm going to write about.

If you're writing about being lost in the House of Mirrors, then after the word *What*, write *lost—House of Mirrors*, or abbreviate with *lost—H of M*. If you're writing about fishing, then write the word *fishing* next on your plan. If you're writing about your first rollercoaster ride, then write *rollercoaster* after the word *What*.

I walk about the room and ask questions if anyone looks as if he or she is stuck. If I see a student writing *Six Flags* but she's really writing about a rollercoaster ride, then I ask a few questions until she decides that her piece is really about the rollercoaster ride, not Six Flags.

Mrs. S.: Would a few writers share what they've written so far on their plans?

Students are usually excited to share their *Who* and *What*. They can see their pieces starting to take shape. I have three or four students share, and then we resume work.

Mrs. S.: Would anyone like to share the *Who* and *What* on your plan?

Sean: My *Who* is *Dad and I*. My *What* is *building a go-cart*.

Max: My *Who* is *my sister and I*. My *What* is *scared in tent*.

Colin: My *Who* is *I*. My *What* is *winning the math challenge*.

Mrs. S.: Please write the word *Where* under the word *What*. When I rode to Shoaff Park, I had to cross St. Joe Road and ride through the woods. So, I have a couple of things to write after the word *Where*.

I'm going to write *St. Joe Rd., woods, Shoaff Park* after *Where*. Again, I'm not writing sentences, just brief notes to myself. If the House of Mirrors was at the 4-H Fair, then write *4-H Fair* after the word *Where*. If your cat had kittens in a box in the laundry room, then write *laundry room* after *Where*. Be specific. Strong writers always use the words or terms that let the audience know exactly where something took place. If you were riding in a hot air balloon from Ft. Wayne to Huntington, then you would write those city names.

Again, I walk around the room making sure everyone is on task and moving right along.

Mrs. S.: Beneath the word *Where*, please write the word *When*. *When* can mean many different things: It could mean last spring, or late at night, or the day after my birthday, or this summer, or right before closing. On my plan, I'm going to write *warm summer day*.

Take a moment and think. When did you do this? Was it last week? Two years ago? In the winter? Right after school started? First thing in the morning? Please write a time that you did this on your plan next to the word *When*.

> On my plans, I put little notes to myself, explaining what I want to say and do in my writing.
>
> — 4th grader

We share a few of the plans again. By now, more students are raising their hands to read. This is a good time to ask questions if we hear anything that confuses us, however, I try to remain silent and give ownership to the students. That way, all of the questions are sincere. The writer is always pleased to answer any queries and revise the plan if it is not clear.

Mrs. S.: Now for the best part—the details. Beneath the word *When*. write a capital *D*. The details will be the interesting parts that no one would know if you didn't add them to your writing. When I rode to Shoaff Park, I had to cross St. Joe Road, which was very busy. So, I'm going to write *#1* under the capital *D* for my first detail. Then, I'll write *St. Joe Rd, busy, waited*. This will remind me that I had to wait and wait until the traffic passed.

Notice that I didn't write a sentence, but just short notes to myself. Now, go back to the event you're writing about. Tell us something that we wouldn't know unless we were there. If you were lost in the House of Mirrors, how did you try to get out? Did you run back and forth? Did you bounce off mirrors? Did you scream for help? Remember, don't write a sentence. Just write a word or two, such as *screamed*. You can add the rest of that detail in your first draft. If you were fishing with your uncle, were you anchored in the middle of a lake? Were you fishing off a pier? Were you standing in waders along the edge of a pond? Write yourself a brief note like *standing in waders*. Now, everybody think back and tell us something specific, something interesting that we'd never know. Please don't write the words *fun* or *scared* or *sad*—we will know how you felt by what you describe. Paint a picture: Tell us something that we can see, hear, touch, smell, or taste. Write that information next to your #1.

I walk around the room and help students when necessary by asking questions. I tell them again to write just a word or two as a reminder. Then, we share a few plans from top to bottom. Our interest is growing—we are investing time in each other's pieces.

Mrs. S.: I'm going to add a second detail to my plan. Please write #2 beneath #1. One of the great things about the day I want to write about is that I had walked through the woods several times on the way to the park, but I'd never ridden my bike through them. The woods had hills that were worn smooth from shoes and bike tires. My bike zoomed up and down the hills. I'm going to write *up and down hills* by my #2. I'll remember to add more information when I write my first draft.

Please add another detail note to your plan—just a word or two. For instance, if you're writing about your cat Muffin having kittens, maybe you'll want to tell us what they looked like as they were born. You might describe how wet their fur looked, how at first they didn't look all that cuddly. You might write *wet fur— slippery* by your #2. Please add another detail note to your plans now.

I walk around the room and read over students' shoulders or offer help through questions. Then, I write #3 on my plan.

Mrs. S.: Please write #3 beneath #2. My last detail is about the little rivulets of water that ran through the woods and emptied into the river. My bike tires would splash through them shooting water up into the air. I'm going to write *tires splash—tiny creeks* by #3.

Now, please add your third detail.

Some students will want to know if they can add one more detail. Some will say they can only think of two details (although that's rare). Both cases are fine. Then, I have two to three students share their plans at this stage.

Mrs. S.: If some of you only have two details, that's fine. Some of you might want to add a fourth or even a fifth detail to complete your plan. Every plan is different. So, please, don't think you must have exactly three details to write a strong personal narrative. Remember your event and write notes for the details you want to share. I will wait two to three minutes while each of you completes your details or reads over the plan you already have.

This is a good time to circulate among students again and read plans over shoulders.

Mrs. S.: Now, we're ready to think about our endings. I know what I want for my ending. I can still remember the feeling when I burst from the woods. My tires hit smooth blacktop and I felt like I was sailing through the park. I want to show that great sense of independence and freedom. Let's all write a capital *E* for Ending under our last detail.

Beside the *E*, I am going to write *smooth blacktop—sailed*. Now, please think about how your event ended. Try to show us with words how you felt. Instead of thinking, *I was happy to see my mom*, think *I ran into my mom's arms, away from the House of Mirrors*. Or instead of thinking, *I was glad because I caught the biggest northern pike*, you might think something like *As I pulled the giant northern pike into the boat, Uncle Ray said, "Mighty fine catch, boy!" I knew he was right—it was the best catch of the day!* You're going to be tempted to write a sentence or two, but don't. Just write yourself a short note about your ending. You'll remember it when you write your first draft.

I walk around the room and assist with questions when necessary. Mostly, I'm reading completed plans over students' shoulders. Many students volunteer to share their entire plans. There is a palpable excitement in the room because we sat and thought and made brief notes. Students feel confident that they can now write these pieces.

Mrs. S.: How many of you are ready to write? *(Typically, all hands shoot into the air.)* How many of you are pleased with what you're going to write? *(Again, almost all hands zoom into the air.)*

As you model more plans, it won't be necessary to share after each addition. However, students sometimes ask to share if we're working in a whole-group setting. They enjoy hearing what everyone is writing, plus they take great pride in the plans they're developing.

My completed plan appears below. *Note:* It is also marked to show the BME structure. See pages 22–23 for more information on *BME.*

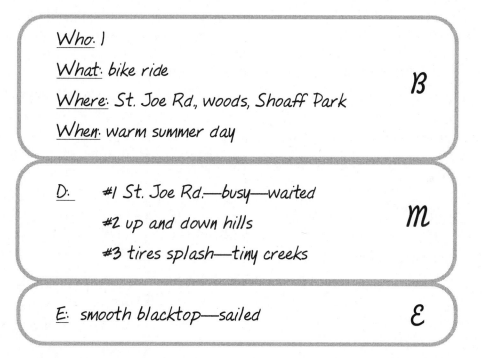

Be prepared! As soon as students have completed their plans, they'll want to write their first drafts. If time allows, please let them continue. Their writing ideas are taking shape and they're ready to go.

From Plan to First Draft

If your day doesn't permit extended writing time, have students save their plans for the next day. Then, before they write, have them sit with a writing buddy. Each partner reads his or her plan aloud two times. During the first reading, the listener becomes familiar with

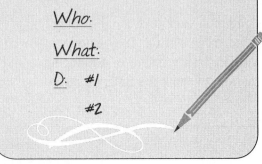

Modifying Plans to Meet Student Needs

No two plans ever look identical. We always need to assess students' writing experiences before demonstrating a plan. Here's a plan that I use with students who are just taking their first steps.

Who:

What:

D: #1

#2

Quick Review of a Simple Plan for Personal Narrative

1. Allow students to write about an emotional event from their lives.

2. Model the different stages of thinking and planning aloud and on the overhead projector.

3. The basic components of the plan for personal narrative are:
   Who
   What
   Where or When (or both)
   D (for Details)
   #1
   #2
   #3
   E (for Ending)

4. Plans for personal narrative can be simpler or more complex, depending on the background of the students and what they want to say.

5. Walk among students during the process to monitor their understanding and progress.

it. During the second reading, the listening partner may pose a question or two about what he or she has heard. In fact, I encourage questions because this helps the writer rethink the piece. It awakens the writer's senses and takes him or her back to the event he or she wants to write about. Also, working with a partner heightens commitment to the writing: now, an audience has heard the plan and wants to read the final piece.

Another strategy to use during partner plan reading is to have the listener celebrate one specific note on the reader's plan. For instance, a student might say, *I heard you say that you "guard the remote." I know exactly what you mean by that. I have to do that at our house, too.* This small amount of feedback is a strong motivator for the writer to stay on task and write the piece.

When students are ready to write from their plans, I write my personal narrative on the overhead projector. I want them to see me refer back to my plan after each addition to my first draft. By doing this, I'm modeling how I want them to use their plans to guide their own writing. It works!

I strongly recommend that students keep their plans out while they draft their pieces. Their plans will help them know what information needs to go in their leads, the middle of their pieces, and the endings. Before they begin to write, we talk about how to divide the plan into these three organizational parts.

Depending on your students' background, you might help them identify the structure of beginning, middle, and ending in their plans with the following method. Ask them to draw a circle or box around the information for *Who, What, Where* and *When*. We label this *B* for the beginning or lead. Next, we draw a circle or box around the details. We label these *M* for the middle. Finally, we draw a circle or box around the *Ending* information. We don't need to label this since it's already labeled. However, sometimes, students enjoy using the letter *E* so they can see *BME* on the page. (See Chapter 4 for more information on the BME structure and story.)

Have I ever had a child create a plan and write something completely different? I certainly have, but thankfully, I can count those incidents on one hand. Teacher modeling is critical. When students watch their teacher create a plan and then write a piece from the plan, this demonstrates the role of the plan and its importance.

A plan will vary according to genre and what the writer wants to accomplish. If a plan is a map, then it should lead the writer through the construction that he or she hopes to create.

The following two plans were created by third-grade students. Even though it was October, this was their first attempt at using a plan before writing. Since this particular classroom had already been immersed in daily writing workshop, students were familiar with the importance of details in personal narrative. I chose a more sophisticated plan

---

Third-Grade Personal Narrative Plans

Abigail's Plan

<u>Who</u>: Amore and I
<u>Where</u>: apartment, Chicago
<u>When</u>: every other weekend
<u>What</u>:
#1 throw his dancing toy
   Detail: jumps and scoots
      paneled floor
#2 he and I cuddle
   Detail: he gets mad
   Detail: I find treats—he cuddles again
#3 out on balcony
   Detail: he's in flower box
   Detail: eats flowers
   Detail: tries to walk ledge
   Detail: lies on radiator
<u>Ending</u>: wish the day would never end

Michael's Plan

<u>Who</u>: Lia and I
<u>Where</u>: house
<u>When</u>: after school, weekends
<u>What</u>:
#1 growl at her
   Detail: hide behind fridge
   Detail: flip her upside down
   Detail: makes me tired
#2 movie with Lia
   Detail: Baby Songs
   Detail: guard the remote
<u>Ending</u>: with Lia more excited than
      ever before

than the one developed in the mini-lesson in this chapter. In these plans, each *What* is a separate event of the narrative. The number of details beneath each *What* was the individual student's choice. They responded eagerly and did a great job!

The purpose of a plan is to help the writer think ahead and know the general framework of what he or she's going to write. It is not meant to be a prison. Quite often, as students are making their plans, they'll ask, "I've thought of something better. Can I change my plan?" My answer is always the same: "Absolutely!" A plan is a tool for thinking. We would never want planning to restrict or confine a writer. In fact, we want the opposite. We want writers to feel free once they have this map or framework. We want to give them the freedom to concentrate on exactly what they want to say and how to say it. They can then add elaboration in their first drafts, painting pictures with words.

As an example, here's the first draft that Michael wrote from his plan (see page 23). Notice that he elaborated on the growl mentioned in his plan by actually adding the sound that he makes. Michael writes about how he flips Lia over his arm and holds her. Finally, instead of telling us about his excitement at the ending, he showed us by painting that emotion with words.

Michael's First Draft

Lia from China and I
    When I get out of school, I play with my little sister from China. I like to flip her upside down, but it makes me very tired when I do it. We mostly play in the living room of our house. Lia wants to be flipped over and over again! I put my right arm behind her back and flip her over like a teacup. Then I bring her right up and hold her.
    Lia is almost two years old. She likes to hide beside the fridge. Then I growl at her like this, "GGGRRRRR!!!!"
    If I hide and growl at the same time, she comes out of hiding! Then I growl at her again and she runs back to her hiding spot.
    When we watch the movie Baby Songs, I try to keep Lia away from the remote! Most of the time she gets it! She tries to grab the remote for any movie of hers.
    Whenever I play with Lia from China, I feel like a tomato plant sprouting in Lia's and my heart!

When to Plan or When Not to Plan

Teachers often ask me, "Should I require a plan from all of my students for the rest of the year?" Quite honestly, the answer is no. I do believe that all students need instruction on how to briefly plan their writing. Again, plans are tools. If a student needs that particular tool, he or she should use it. If not, I hope the student doesn't. Why should someone waste valuable time writing a detailed plan if he or she can organize mentally? I would rather see a student writing and revising than completing an unnecessary task. But how can we tell whether a student would benefit from making a plan?

One of the byproducts of a plan is that the writing remains organized. As the writing progresses to a satisfying end, it's easy to identify organizational features such as these:

- *Does the lead provide a lure that entices the reader to engage in the text?*
- *Does the lead offer necessary information to set up the writing?*
- *Does the text advance in a logical order?*
- *Are there transitions that pull the reader from one idea to another?*
- *Does the reader feel an urgency to continue reading through the text?*
- *Does the writer sequence information and ideas so they build on one another?*
- *Does the ending pull the piece together and satisfy the reader?*

If a student chooses not to plan on paper, but his or her writing is disorganized, then intervene and create a plan together with that child.

Graphic Organizers vs. Original Plans

Much earlier in my teaching career, I would copy the graphic organizers that came with published pre-writing materials. Some students were successful with these tools, while they seemed to send others into a state of panic. It didn't take long for me to realize that many students thought there was only *one* correct answer to put in each of those ovals or squares or on those lines. I believe those pre-arranged sheets gave them the message that they were jumping into the middle of something, but they weren't sure what it was.

The few times that my students used graphic organizers, it taught me another valuable lesson. After all their work, several students never referred to the organizers as they wrote. In other words, they didn't realize they had been thinking through something that they wanted to write. Instead, students thought they'd completed one activity, and now it was time to move on to writing.

This isn't the case when students create original plans. They know that they're thinking through their own pieces and making notes to guide them as they write. The plan makes sense to students because they made the plans from nothing. It's part of the writing process.

Another byproduct of making a plan is that the writing remains focused—it stays true to purpose and topic. As you saw, Michael's first draft shows focus. All of his writing remains on the topic of his sister Lia and himself.

If you observe a student planning internally, with no notes on paper, and his or her writing is focused and carries meaning, he or she probably doesn't need a plan. However, if you observe a student writing, and the work is not focused, it's a strong indicator that he or she would benefit from making and following a plan. Again, I would intervene.

Some students realize they need a written plan for some genres and not for others. For instance, many students can write personal narratives or poetry without a written plan. But when they decide to write a story, they learn that a simple plan can make the journey more enjoyable.

Some students enjoy the planning process so much that they continue it all year long. Others internalize the organization of writing and do well by planning mentally before they write. Some students continue to use a written plan for lengthier works but pre-write mentally for shorter pieces. Our job is to demonstrate the process of planning and to help students understand what works best for them.

Chapter 3 Review

- Model many different kinds of plans.
- During the planning process, invite students to share their developing plans.
- Students may share plans with a writing partner to refine their ideas and purpose.
- Teachers may want students to show the organization of BME on their plans.
- No two plans are ever identical; their designs are dictated by idea, purpose, audience, and form.
- Not all students need to make a written plan for each piece they write.

Chapter 4

Organizing for Story

Reading and writing story is an emphasis in all grades 2–4 classrooms. Story, whether real-life or fictional, has two basic structures. We want students to know that every story has a clear beginning, middle, and ending. We also want them to be able to identify the story characteristics of character, problem, setting, conflict or struggle, and resolution. A story doesn't have one or the other; it must have both.

It's better to introduce one structure and then the other. However, if you would ask me which structure should be taught first, I'd have a difficult time choosing. Kindergartners can easily be taught to identify characters and problems and their struggles to overcome those problems. They also can tell you which action begins a story, which action ends the story, and list all the middle actions.

So where do we begin? Since many other writing forms have the beginning, middle, and ending design, I like to begin with the characteristics that make story distinct. I read many stories to students that have likable characters with believable problems or struggles. In story, I want the protagonist to be actively engaged and the resolution to make sense and be satisfying to the reader. I believe that simpler stories make the best examples. I want the structure to appear uncluttered to students as they read like writers.

Framing a Story

If we help students identify story traits in the books they read, it will be much easier for them to make successful story plans. To introduce students to the characteristics of a story, I like to use *Oliver Finds His Way* by Phyllis Root as an example. By asking a series of questions, I reveal the frame of the story to students. I write the following questions and responses on an overhead projector or chart paper.

> ### Stories with Clear Structure
>
> - *Don't Laugh, Joe* by Keiko Kasza
> - *Jessica* by Kevin Henkes
> - *The Legend of the Lady Slipper* by Lise Lunge-Larsen and Margi Preus
> - *Mole Music* by David McPhail
> - *Oliver Finds His Way* by Phyllis Root
> - *Owen* by Kevin Henkes
> - *The Paper Bag Princess* by Robert Munsch
> - *Tippy-Toe Chick, Go!* by George Shannon

Questions	Student Responses
Who is this story about? (character)	Oliver the bear
What is his problem? (problem)	He gets lost.
Where does the story take place? (setting)	outside
When does it take place? (setting)	a fall day
What does Oliver try to do to find his way home? (conflict/struggle)	He tries to find the twisty tree and and clumpy bush.
That doesn't work. What does he try next? (conflict/struggle)	He cries and cries and cries.
That doesn't help. What does he try next? (conflict/struggle)	He thinks and thinks and thinks.
What does he try next? (conflict/struggle)	He roars and roars and roars.
How does this story end? (ending)	Oliver roars so loudly that his mom and dad hear him and roar back. Oliver follows the sound of their roars back home.

I recommend framing several stories so your students can really grasp the basic traits of story. Once they can easily recognize these features in published stories, they are much more dutiful about placing them in their own writing. Plus, the whole-group practice establishes background vocabulary and understanding of this story structure among all students. They can now be good writing buddies who hold each other accountable for these traits during the planning and writing of their own stories.

Quick Review: Framing a Story

1. Select a simple story that contains all the story traits (character, problem, setting, at least three events—problems/conflicts—and resolution).
2. Leading up to this experience, read the story at least twice to students—more is even better—but not at one sitting.
3. Ask questions so students can identify the main story traits.
4. Record students' responses on an overhead or chart paper so the framing can be used as support when they create their own story plans.

Finding Beginning, Middle, and Ending

I also use published stories to show students the BME structure. Like framing a story, this process involves asking questions about the story. I scribe on chart paper or on the overhead as students provide answers to my questions. Here is an example of the process using the same story, *Oliver Finds His Way*.

Teacher Questions and Comments	Student Responses
What is the first thing that Oliver does in this story?	He chases a big yellow leaf.
That's the beginning action of the story.	
Emily, will you mark that sentence with a capital *B*?	Student writes capital *B* next to sentence: He chases a big yellow leaf. B
Now let's go to the end of the story.	
What's the last thing that Oliver does?	He runs to his very own house.
That's the ending action of our story. Let's mark it with a capital *E*.	Student writes capital *E* next to sentence: He runs to his very own house. E
Now, let's go back to the beginning, right after the first action. Tell me each thing that Oliver does in the story. (Use the book as a guide.)	Oliver looks for the leaf. M Oliver looks for his parents. M Oliver calls for his parents. M He runs to a tree. M He runs to a bush. M He cries and cries some more. M He rubs his nose and thinks. M He roars and roars and roars. M He hears his mama and papa. M Oliver roars back. M
Now, we need to mark each of those with a capital *M* for middle actions.	Students write a capital *M* beside each middle action.
There's one beginning action and one ending action. How many middle actions are there in this story?	10

At this point, I would explain that not all stories have ten actions but that the middle always has at least three actions. (Actually, I refer to this story structure as BMMME because I want students to remember that the middle has at least three actions, if not more.) I would go on to say: *As you write stories, remember that the middle of the story is where the character is involved in a struggle or conflict. That development requires three actions or more to make it believable since most problems cannot be solved in one try.*

If you're working on chart paper, you can cut apart the ending action and rearrange the lines so that they appear in the same order as they do in the book. If you're working on the overhead, you can erase the ending line and rewrite it at the bottom. The reason I like to find the beginning action first and the ending second is that students can then concentrate on identifying the middle actions without worry about the ending.

Quick Review: Finding BME

1. Select a simple story that has a clearly delineated BME.
2. Leading up to this experience, read that story to your students at least two times—more is better—but not at one sitting.
3. Ask students to identify the first action—the first thing that happens.
4. Write an abbreviated account for students, and have a child write a large *B* by this action to identify the beginning of the story.
5. Ask students to identify the last action—the last thing that happens.
6. Record this action, and have a student label it with a large *E* to identify the ending of the story.
7. Return to the beginning of the story, and ask students what happens next.
8. Write an abbreviated account of that, and have a student label it with a large *M* to identify part of the middle.
9. Continue with the questions until all the middle actions have been identified and labeled with a capital *M*.
10. Sequence the three parts of the story. Then, ask students to count the middle actions.
11. Post this chart in the room as a resource.

Mini-Lesson: Real-Life Stories

I think it's easier for students to plan and write a real-life story before attempting a fictional story. I also think it's helpful to guide them in writing a simple story for younger readers before they tackle something more complex. It's a great motivator.

Writing a story for a younger audience is a strategy that I like to use with students in grades 2–4. I first get them excited about writing stories for our kindergarten or first-grade friends, who will be appreciative audiences. I often share with students that these children need lively, short stories to keep them excited about reading. My students are always eager to begin their stories.

First, we examine many of the emergent and early fluent classroom stories marketed by educational

Stories for the Youngest Reader

These titles are ideal to examine for simple story structures.

- *Baron: Rescue Dog* by Lola M. Schaefer
- *Coyote Plants a Peach Tree* by Mary L. Brown
- *The Hungry Sea Star* by Sherry Shahan
- *Little Puffer Fish* by Amany F. Hassanein
- *Nothing in the Mailbox* by Carolyn Ford

publishers. We see how only 80–120 words can make a satisfying story. Next, we create simple story plans, beginning with the identification of a character. Quite often, I ask students to brainstorm a list of backyard animals. They usually name dogs, cats, snakes, rabbits, squirrels, blue jays, moles, skunks, and so on. Then, I suggest they select one of these animals for their story character. I also recommend that it be an animal with which they are familiar.

While students create their original story plans at their desks, I create my own at the overhead projector. (See page 34 for completed plan.) Here is how I guide students through this plan.

Mrs. S.: Let's begin our story plans by writing the abbreviation *CHAR* for the word *character* at the top of our papers. I'm going to select the squirrel as my character so I will write that after the abbreviation for *character* on my plan. Go ahead and select the animal you want to write about. Would anyone like to share his or her character with us?

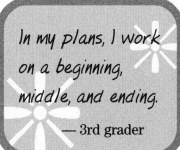

In my plans, I work on a beginning, middle, and ending.

— 3rd grader

Grace: Mine's a mouse.

Lola: My character is a cat.

Jon: I'm writing about a snake.

Mrs. S.: Great! Now, I need to brainstorm a few problems my squirrel can have. I want to keep my squirrel in the natural world, so these will need to be real-life problems. Let's see. Squirrel may try to build a nest, but outside forces keep taking it apart. Or a cooper's hawk is roosting nearby, and squirrel needs to find a safe place to hide. Or squirrel feels cold air and knows that she needs to store food for winter. While I'm thinking about which problem I want to use, let's all write the word *problem* underneath the abbreviation for *character* on our plans.

Four common problems an animal might face are escaping from a predator, finding food, preparing a nest or a place to have babies, and getting back home safely. I'll give you all a few moments to think of two or three problems that your character might face. Each problem in the story must create a struggle or conflict that your character will have to work to resolve. (*I pause a few seconds to think of a problem.*) I've decided to use the problem of building a nest. I'll write the words *build nest* next to the word *problem*. As soon as you've decided on a problem for your character, please write a short note beside the word *problem* on your plan.

Leaving my plan on the overhead, I walk around the room for three or four minutes and read plans over students' shoulders. If someone needs help, I'll stop and ask questions, such as:

- *I see you selected a dog as your character. Is your dog lost or is it chasing another animal?*

- *You've chosen a cat as your character. Beside* problem *you've written* scared. *What is frightening your cat?*

- *I can see that your character is a blue jay. After* problem, *you've written the word* nest. *Is your bird trying to build a nest or has another bird taken the nest it built?*

Then, I return to the overhead projector.

Mrs. S.:   I am going to add the word *setting* to my plan beneath the word *problem*. Setting refers to two things: place and time. I want to make sure the setting increases the urgency of the problem and the character's struggle. My story will take place in my backyard, and the time will be spring. I want it to be spring because that is when squirrels have their babies. I want my readers to care that my squirrel will get her nest built in time. I'm placing my story in a backyard because there may or may not be good nest building materials there. I'll add those two notes to my plan like this: I'll write *P* for *place*. After the *P*, I'll write *my backyard*. Then, I'll write *T* for *time*. After the *T*, I'll write *spring*.

Now, I'd like you to decide where your story will take place. Will it happen in the woods? In your backyard? At the park? In the basement? Under the eaves of the house? In the garden? Make a choice, and write that next to a capital *P* for *place*. (*I pause to allow students to fill in the place.*)

You have one more decision. What is the time of your story? Time can mean a season like summer or winter, or it can mean morning or evening. It could even be more specific, like the Fourth of July. Think about your problem. What time would be believable? Also, think about how the time can add to the tension of your story. Why would your character need to solve the problem quickly at this time? After you've made a decision add a capital *T* to your plan for *time*, and write a note about the time of the story.

Again, I travel around the room, making sure that students understand how the plan is developing. If they need assistance, I ask questions. Then, I return to the overhead projector.

Mrs. S.:   Since we all know that a story starts when something happens, I need to think about what action will bring my audience into my story. I want squirrel to be making a nest high in a cottonwood tree. She is bringing many twigs and old leaves to the limb where she's building her nest. These actions are called the *events* of the story. First, I'll write the word *Events* on my plan beneath the word *setting*. Students, please add that word to your plans, too. (*Teachers, you can label this part of the plan Struggle, Conflict, or Events, whatever you choose.*)

When the story begins, I want the squirrel to be making her nest, I'll write *#1* below *Events* and then the words *making nest*. I'll also go ahead and write *#2* underneath that for my next action.

I'd like all of you to think about what your character will be doing when the story begins. After you make that decision, write a brief note to yourselves next to *#1* on your plan. Please, don't write sentences.

I walk about the room as students add the first action to their plans. Before continuing with more actions, it's a good idea to have three or four students share how they are going to begin their stories. If students are struggling, they may hear an idea that will help them move forward with their plan. Then, I return to the overhead projector.

Mrs. S.: Remember, we're writing these stories for young readers, so keep them simple and easily understandable. Since we want the events to pose a problem to our character, things will get worse before they get better. I know that squirrels build their nests in early spring, so I'm going to have a horrible windstorm in the night blow away everything that squirrel has assembled for her nest. By #2, I'll write *wind destroys nest*. I'll also go ahead and add #3 to my list of events.

Students, think about what could happen that would make your character have to work hard or struggle. Will he look for food and not find it? Will he try to find a hiding place from an enemy? Is he trying to outrun some kind of danger? Remember, we want things to get a little worse—not really bad yet— just a little worse. When you've decided on a great second action, go ahead and add that to your plan and then write #3 under #2.

I walk around the room to trouble-shoot. Most students will have their own ideas about what needs to happen next in their stories, but a few will need questions to think it through. I usually have two or three different students who volunteer to share their plans from beginning to end. The more story ideas that students hear, the better equipped they are to construct story independently later during writer's workshop.

Mrs. S.: Now, I want my squirrel to work for days rebuilding the nest. It's almost complete when she runs out of twigs and leaves. She has to hunt and hunt to find enough materials to finish her nest. She will actually use some leftover straw from the garden and some cabbage leaves that have wilted over the winter. Beside #3, I'll write *rebuilds nest—almost complete—can't find twigs and leaves—garden*. Then, I'll add #4 to my list of events.

Remember, you want your problem to get just a little worse. You want your character to work hard—to struggle—to solve the problem. What else could grow wrong for your character?

Again, I travel around the room, checking that students are staying on track, asking questions where needed. I will also ask for new volunteers to share their entire plans. By now, the tension is building in the stories, and students are intrigued by how others are making a story.

Mrs. S.: My story is almost complete. I want one more little problem for my squirrel. It helps develop your stories if you can think of at least three hurdles that your character has to overcome. Three or more mini-problems create the struggle or conflict that builds tension in your stories. *(I pause a few seconds to think.)* I want my squirrel to complete her nest, but while she goes to gather bird feathers to make it soft, another squirrel tries to claim the nest. So, beside my #4 I will write *another squirrel claims nest*.

Students, choose the last hurdle or mini-problem for your character. What else goes wrong before we move into the ending? Add this problem to your plan by #4.

I travel around the room and read plans over students' shoulders or question those writers who might be stuck. By now though, students are usually into their stories and adding another obstruction doesn't seem that difficult. As before, ask for two or three volunteers to share their developing plans.

Note: What should you do if a student has developed a good plan but only has two obstacles for the character? Flow with it. This demonstrates that that child has developed as a writer. Maybe his or her story will work better with an opening action, two obstacles, and then an ending. The purpose of the plan is to help students organize and remain focused. We don't need to put undue pressure on them as they develop stories.

Mrs. S.:   Now, it's time to decide how we would like our stories to end. Endings need to be believable. They need to bubble out of the story, make sense, and satisfy the reader.

My squirrel needs her nest because her babies are ready to be born. But she has a day or so before that happens. I want her to start a new nest, a nest for the squirrel that is claiming hers. My final scene will be squirrel with her babies in her nest. The other squirrel will be in her new nest on the other side of tree. On my plan, I'm going to write a capital *E* for *ending*. Beside the *E*, I'll write *helps build new nest—births babies—warm & safe*.

Students, it's your turn. It's time for the endings of your stories. Write a short note or two to yourself about how you want your story to end.

For the last time, I move around the room. Most students are anxious to share how their characters will solve their problems. As a class, we share two to four plans from top to bottom, and the process is complete.

This is what my final story plan looks like.

<u>CHAR</u>: SQUIRREL

<u>PROBLEM</u>: BUILD NEST

<u>SETTING</u>:   P = my backyard

   T = spring

<u>EVENTS</u>:   (1.) making nest

   (2.) wind destroys nest

   (3.) rebuilds nest—almost complete—

   can't find twigs and leaves—garden

   (4.) another squirrel claims nest

<u>E</u>: Helps build new nest—births babies—warm & safe

Reading Plans to a Partner

It helps students internalize, and sometimes revise, their plans if they have an opportunity to share their work with a writing partner. As I discussed in Chapter 3 on personal narrative plans, I like to place students in pairs. Each partner reads his plan two times to the listening partner. The listener then repeats the gist of the plan back to the writer. If the listener has any questions or is confused by any of the plan, this is the time to ask the writer questions. Sometimes, as the writer reads his plan, he or she will think of a way to improve the story. Quite often, I see pencils moving as students add new events or a different ending. After one set of readings is complete, the other partner has an opportunity to read his or her plan.

Story is a compelling genre for students to write. First, show them the two structures of character, problem, setting, events, solution, and BME in published work. Then, help them plan their own short stories. I always tell teachers that students need to design several (four to six) story plans as a whole group to learn the process behind story development; it's not important that they write a story for each plan. We want students to learn these organizational tools so they can express themselves through story whenever they choose.

Quick Review: Plan a Real-Life Story

1. Model each step at the overhead projector or on chart paper.
2. Help students identify a character and record it on their plan.
3. Show them how to identify a believable problem for the character. Record the problem on the plan.
4. Record the setting for the story, both time and place.
5. Decide on a beginning action—something that starts the story—and record it.
6. Continue by selecting and recording three actions that move the story along. These events should increase the tension or struggle in the story.
7. Record how the story ends. The ending needs to make sense and follow naturally from the other actions.

Second-Grade Plan and Story

This plan and story were written by Jordyn, a second grader.

Character: Amy and dog
Problem: can't find her dog
Setting: Amy's house
Events:

1. looks under her bed—not there

2. looks in closet—not there

3. looks in box in laundry room—not there

E: finds her—she has puppies

The Surprise

Once there was a girl named Amy. She had a dog named Cassie. Amy could not find Cassie. She looked under her bed. Cassie was not there. She looked in the closet. She was not there. She looked in the laundry room. She was not there. She looked in her mom's room. Cassie was under her mom's blanket! Guess what? She had eight puppies! Five of them were girls. Two of them were brown and white. The other three were black and brown. The three boys were all black and brown. One of the boy puppies had a white spot on his head. Amy named him Spot. Amy named one of the girls, Princess. Amy got to keep Cassie, Spot, and Princess.

Chapter 4 Review

- Students learn story traits by framing published stories.
- Students recognize the BME story structure by studying published literature.
- Model and plan a real-life story while students make their own plans for original stories.
- Allow students to share their plans with writing partners.

Chapter 5

Organizing for Poetry

A s with all forms of writing, the best preparation for writing poetry is reading poetry. Students need to hear at least one, if not three, poems a day to feel the rhythm and emotion that is specific to poetry. Ideally, they should always have access to books of poetry to find the poems that speak to them.

I enjoy watching students discover the beauty and efficiency of this form. And, as soon as they learn that poetry need not rhyme, they are set loose in a wonderful world of words, meaning, and, sometimes, metaphor.

Poetry, because of its brevity, is one form of writing that requires little or no physical planning. However, I always insist that students think before they write. I tell them: *Know what you want to say before you try to say it.* For some students, those words are all that's necessary. They can organize their poetic thoughts and put pencil to paper. Other students need that initial brainstorming and organizational time to pinpoint the meaning they're seeking.

Mini-Lesson: Modeling a Brainstorming Plan

For most students in grades 2–4, I suggest using a web as a way to both brainstorm and then organize their chosen details into a poem. Again, I would advise modeling your own plan for a poem. In the following mini-lesson, I show students my thoughts about the development of a poem about redbud trees.

Mrs. S.: Today, I noticed the redbud blossoms floating in the air. I love them. They are so tiny, yet there are so many of them. I stopped for a few minutes and just watched. I'm going to make a web so that later I can write a poem about what I saw. In my center oval, I'm going to write the topic of my poem—*redbud*.

I place a transparency on the overhead projector. I draw an oval in the center of the page and then write *redbud* in it.

Mrs. S.: Now, I'll think of details and images. First of all, the branches of the redbud tree were covered with thousands of tiny flowers. On my web, I'm going to add *branches covered*.

I draw an oval, write *branches covered* inside, and connect it to the redbud oval.

Mrs. S.: When the wind blew, it carried hundreds of blossoms away, but it looked as if the flowers were flying. I'm going to add *blossoms fly* to my web.

I draw another oval, write *blossoms fly* inside, and connect it to the redbud oval.

Mrs. S.: I always know that warm weather is coming soon when the redbud tree blooms. It means spring is really here. I'll add the word *spring* to my web, too.

I repeat the process for adding an oval with the word *spring* to the web.

Mrs. S.: When I examined the redbud flowers closely, I saw just how small and dainty they were. *Dainty petals* describes that well. I'll add it to my web.

I repeat the process for adding an oval with the words *dainty petals* to the web.

Mrs. S.: I love their color. It's not just purple and not just red, but a combination. I'll write my own word *purple-red* on the web.

I add an oval with the word *purple-red* to the web.

Mrs. S.: And something that always amazes me about the redbud is that it flowers before it buds with leaves. The flowers are the only life on the bare branches. I'll add the words *no leaves* to the web, too.

I add an oval with the words *no leaves* to the web.

Mrs. S.: I'm going to stop now. This is most of what I observed. I'm going to let these words simmer for a moment until I decide how I want to write my poem. I probably won't use all of these observations in the final poem, but it's a good set to consider.

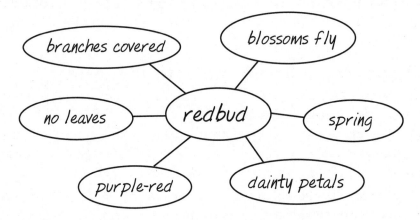

Mrs. S.: Today, all of you will make a web for a poem. Take a moment to look through your writer's notebooks to see if you've made notes on something this year that you'd like to describe in a poem.

I give the students six to eight minutes to browse through their notebooks. Then, I ask them if they have found any ideas. I do this so those who may be feeling a little confused can see what other students are selecting.

Mrs. S.: Has anyone found something that they might like to share?

Kyle: I want to write about clouds. I've written some notes in here on the different shapes and colors of clouds.

Joel: Remember when we made entries in our notebooks the day it snowed? I'm going to use that idea of a new snowfall for a poem.

Mekhi: My dog. I've got so many notes in here about how my dog looks at different times of the day.

Mrs. S.: I'm pleased to hear that you're finding ideas for poems in your notebooks.

This might be all you accomplish on the first day, but by now, students are usually excited about taking the next step of making their own webs. Here's how I guide them in creating their webs.

Mrs. S.: Let's see how many details you can brainstorm for your poem. I'd like each of you to make your own web. Please write your topic in an oval in the center of your paper. Since these are description poems, you can brainstorm details of how your topic looks, feels, smells, tastes, makes sound, or what it does. Take one simple detail and make a short note—just one or two words—and add it to your web.

I continue this process, stopping every so often to give students opportunities to share what they've written. I try to limit the size of webs for poetry to about six or eight details. That's plenty to find one image to develop in a poem.

> *I plan as I go. I think, write, then reread. I do that over and over again.* — 2nd grader

Poetry Books That Inspire the Writer

Just for Teachers

I'm always surprised to learn how many teachers are hesitant to write poetry with their students. Read any or all of these titles to give yourself the confidence to enjoy poetry with your class.

- *Awakening the Heart* by Georgia Heard
- *For the Good of the Earth and Sun* by Georgia Heard
- *Kid's Poems: Teaching Second Graders to Love Writing Poetry* by Regie Routman
- *Kid's Poems: Teaching Third and Fourth Graders to Love Writing Poetry* by Regie Routman
- *Poetry Matters* by Ralph Fletcher

Here are a few of the titles that I like to share with students.

- *all the small poems* by Valerie Worth
- *Earthshake: Poems from the Ground Up* by Lisa Westberg Peters
- *Fireflies at Midnight* by Marilyn Singer
- *Lives: Poems About Famous Americans* selected by Lee Bennett Hopkins
- *A Lucky Thing* by Alice Schertle
- *Old Elm Speaks* by Kristine O'Connell George
- *Summersaults* by Douglas Florian
- *Swing Around the Sun* by Barbara Juster Esbensen
- *This Place I Know: Poems of Comfort* selected by Georgia Heard

Second-Grade Poetry Plans

Here are two different webs and poems written by second graders.

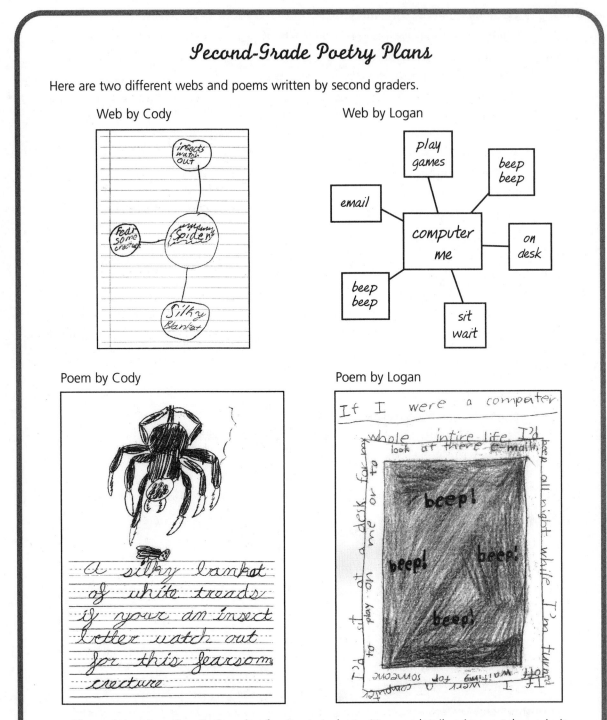

Web by Cody

Web by Logan

Poem by Cody

Poem by Logan

The web is a non-threatening plan for most students. No one detail or image takes priority over another. Students add each detail or image as they think of it. Later, they can reread their webs and select the couple of details or images that fit together for their poetic thoughts. Again, some students will rely on the web for every poem they write. Others will begin to brainstorm and organize in their minds. Our job is to model the use of the web and present it as a tool for students' use.

On another day, I model writing the first draft of a poem from my web.

Mrs. S.: I've been thinking about my redbud web. I have many good details listed. Today, I want to reread those details and select a few that I can organize into a poem. Poets usually take one image or one scene and develop it into a thought that's unusual. A poet looks at the usual in an unusual way. *(I stop to think for a few seconds.)* I'm going to write about how the purple-red branches scatter the blossoms and they fly away. I like the form of haiku when I'm writing about nature. So, that's the form I'm going to use.

I place my web on the overhead projector and think out loud as I choose images. Of course, I'm constantly revising, scratching out words or images and replacing them with others. Students always want to offer lines. However, I politely explain that writing this poem is a personal experience and that I prefer they remain silent bystanders and allow me to select the words I need.

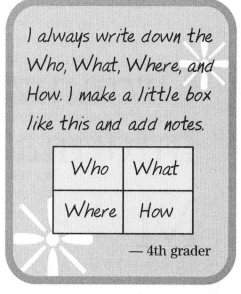

I always write down the Who, What, Where, and How. I make a little box like this and add notes.

Who	What
Where	How

— 4th grader

After several revisions, I eventually produced this haiku.

Purple-red branches
scatter springtime confetti—
Petal-wings, away!

Chapter 5 Review

- Read published poems to your students daily.
- A web is a good brainstorming and organizational tool for planning poetry.
- Use a web to model your thinking and planning for a poem.
- Coach students as they develop their own webs.
- Model writing a poem using some of the information from your web.

Chapter 6

Organizing for Information Writing

Many students enjoy writing about what they know and what they're learning. The world is filled with information that makes them marvel. Because there are so many different kinds of information writing, such as biographies, historical accounts, newspaper and magazine articles, and procedures and directions, it makes sense that the form of the information writing drives the plan.

Mini-Lesson: Organization That Engages Readers

Authors organize material in information books in many different ways. For instance, in the biography *When Marian Sang*, Pam Munoz Ryan writes about events centered around Marian Anderson's love of music. Sneed B. Collard III lists general information about many animals in *Animal Dads* and then presents an example that gives specific details of one particular animal. In *Pick, Pull, Snap! Where Once a Flower Bloomed*, I present information about the growing season of different plants in a circular structure, beginning and ending in early spring. This structure works well with cycles like the growing season.

Some information books incorporate timelines that take readers back in time. The following mini-lesson shows how *On This Spot: An Expedition Back Through Time* by Susan Goodman does this, and students' response to this organizational tool.

Mrs. S.: Remember this book, *On This Spot: An Expedition Back Through Time*? Who can remind us what this book is about?

Ariel: It starts right now in New York City. Each time you turn the page you go back in time to the same place, but a lot of years have passed.

Mrs. S.: That was an excellent summary of the book. Thank you. How many of you remember some of the information that was in this book?

Gilbert: We learned that New York City used to be called New Amsterdam. And people from different countries lived there.

Austin: A long time ago there weren't any buildings, and mammoths lived there.

Mary: Before that, there was only ice. There weren't any buildings or animals, just ice.

Ariel: Native Americans lived there, too. Only it wasn't a city, it was a forest.

Mrs. S.: You're remembering a lot of information. Did it seem like the author hopped around and wrote these facts as she remembered them?

Devin: No. She had a plan.

Mary: The numbers at the top of the page told us how long ago it was.

Jaime: Every time you turned the page, she took you farther back in time.

Mrs. S.: So, there was some organization to the book.

Students: Yes!

Mrs. S.: If I understand you correctly, the author organized her information in a timeline from present to the distant past. Did you like that part of the book?

Devin: Yes! It was like we were time traveling.

Jaime: She showed us how the land changed over millions of years.

Austin: I liked reading how many years ago at the top.

Mrs. S.: We can use that organizational tool in our own writing. We could use a timeline to write about the life of a star in the sky or an underground cave. We could start with the present and work backward, telling our audience what was happening a hundred, five hundred, a thousand, or even ten thousand years ago. If we decided to write about ourselves, we could go back one year at a time and write what we were doing or how we looked.

To help us remember this organizational tool, let's make a note about it in our writer's notebooks. This is what I'm going to write: *Sometimes, I might want to organize my information writing by starting at the present and working backward in time.* I'll give you a moment to make your own notes.

Note: Never attempt a mini-lesson like this unless you have read the non-fiction book at least once, preferably twice to your students. Also, I recommend only discussing one book a day with them.

For a mini-lesson on *So You Want to Be President?*, I lead students into the discovery that Judith St. George organized her information around one topic—facts about past presidents of the United States. She has two ways of engaging the reader: She speaks directly to the reader, and she organizes her information around interesting facts about presidential pets, bathtubs, home states, dances, sports, and ages. The short introduction and conclusion act like bookends, holding the other pieces of information in place. Then, I brainstorm other topics students could write using this same kind of organization. *Note:* Always remember to provide time for students to make a note about each different organizational structure in their writer's notebooks.

> ## Books for Non-fiction Study
>
> - *Animal Dads* by Sneed B. Collard III
> - *On This Spot: An Expedition Back Through Time* by Susan Goodman
> - *Pick, Pull, Snap! Where Once a Flower Bloomed* by Lola M. Schaefer
> - *So You Want to Be President?* by Judith St. George
> - *When Marian Sang* by Pam Munoz Ryan

For a biography like *When Marian Sang*, I would model an entry like this for my notebook: *I might organize information around a series of events. I could start with the first thing that happens in the process and then add other examples as they happen. This might be especially helpful in writing biographies.*

Using a factual science book such as *Animal Dads*, I'd share the following notebook entry with students: *List general information and then add specific details about one particular example.*

As you and your students examine different informational texts, you may want to create a classroom chart. List the book title, author, and the kind of organization that students discover (written in their language). Leave space on the chart for a volunteer to write an example from the text. Post the chart in your classroom to provide ongoing support for student writers.

After students have examined and identified different organizational styles in informational text, they are well-equipped to plan the organization of their own pieces.

Different Plans for Different Forms

A writer needs to know the idea, purpose, audience, and form before planning his or her writing. For instance, if a student is writing a piece on general knowledge about zebras, the plan might look like this.

What: zebras

Focus: adaptation to environment

Details:

    1. coloring and markings

    2. hooves and speed

    3. teeth and eating habits

    4. survival

Ending: how long they have lived on planet

On the other hand, if a student was going to write an informational piece on the water cycle, his or her plan might look something like this.

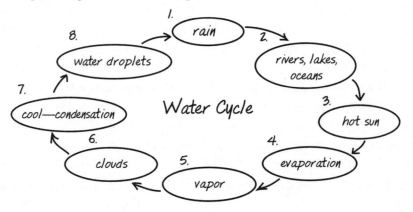

A student who wants to write about animals in Antarctica might use the bookend approach. For the beginning, he or she would ask a question to introduce the piece: *What animals can hunt and breed in the frozen world of Antarctica?* In the middle, the student could list animals like seals, penguins, killer whales, and petrels, and the individual behaviors or physical traits that help them survive in the cold climate. At the end, he or she would close with another question: *Do you have what it takes to live and survive in Antarctica?* The final plan might look like this:

B: question about Antarctica
M: details about:
    seals
    penguins
    killer whales
    petrels
E: question for the audience

A Second Grader's Informational Plan and First Draft

Here's a plan and the first draft for a simple informational piece on the brain. This student's purpose for writing was to show what she had learned as part of her health study.

Plan by Tait, second grade

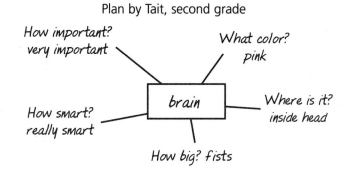

Brain by Tait

Do you know what is an important part of your body? It is your brain. What color is a brain? Well, a brain is pink. How big is a brain? Right now, it's about the size of your two fists. But your brain grows as you get bigger. Where is your brain? Well, let me tell you where it is. It is inside your head. How smart is your brain? Your brain is smart. Do you want to know how smart? It is so smart it knows everything. It knows so much. You know everything that it knows about reading and writing. What does your brain do on the right? It does art and crafts. What does it do on the left? It does something good. It does school work like math, reading, writing, and thinking. That is what I've learned about the brain.

The effectiveness of the written plan is that it forces students to slow down and think about the writing. By taking the time to create external order, they automatically organize their own thinking.

Again, always model any new plan that you introduce to students. It's your thorough, step-by-step explanation that insures understanding and success on their part. And remember that plans, even for nonfiction, are brief. Plans work as maps or frameworks to organize students' thinking and guide them through their first drafts.

Chapter 6 Review

- The kind of plan for information writing is determined by the choice of form.
- Most plans will include topic, focus, and details.
- Always model how to use any new plans you introduce.
- Like all other plans, the plan for an information piece is brief.

Final Thoughts: Freedom to Write

Slow down, stop, and reflect. That's what we're showing students when we take the time to think before putting pen to paper or fingers to keyboard. Crafting thoughtful text takes patience and hard work. A written plan demands concentration from the writer. It forces him or her to think: *What do I want to write? Why do I want to write this? Who am I writing this for? How will I write it?* Once the writer has answered these basic questions about idea, purpose, audience, and form, the piece begins to take shape. Attention and thought can then be given to the actual craft of writing.

There's great freedom in knowing what you want to write and the order in which you'll write it. A written plan allows a comfortable setting in which an author can experiment with language. The writer's mind is not torn between multiple jobs. He or she has the time and energy to play with leads, descriptions, details, and endings.

> When I plan a story, I decide on a problem and 3–4 events that I want to happen.
>
> — 3rd grader

Students themselves tell me over and over again that making a plan helps them think and write better. If planning supports students during the process, be sure to model and encourage its use. See where this organizational tool can take them. Watch your students grow into independent thinkers and writers.

Bibliography

Adler, David A.. "Cam Jensen Mysteries." New York: Penguin Putnam Books for Young Readers.

Arnold, Caroline. *Australian Animals.* New York: HarperCollins, 2000.

Arnold, Caroline. *Birds: Nature's Magnificent Flying Machines.* Watertown, MA: Charlesbridge Publishing, 2003.

Arnold, Caroline. *Lion.* New York: HarperCollins, 1995.

Brown, Mary L. *Coyote Plants a Peach Tree.* Katonah, NY: Richard C. Owen Publishers, Inc., 1996.

Collard III, Sneed B. *Animal Dads.* Boston: Houghton Mifflin, 1997.

Dorn, Linda J. and Carla Soffos. *Scaffolding Young Writers: A Writers' Workshop Approach.* Portland, ME: Stenhouse Publishers, 2001.

Esbensen, Barbara Juster. *Swing Around the Sun.* Minneapolis, MN: Carolrhoda Books, Inc., 1965, 2003.

Fletcher, Ralph. *Live Writing: Breathing Life into Your Words.* New York: Avon Books, 1999.

Fletcher, Ralph. *Poetry Matters.* New York: HarperCollins Publishers, Inc., 2002.

Fletcher, Ralph and JoAnn Portalupi. *Writing Workshop: The Essential Guide.* Portsmouth, NH: Heinemann, 2001.

Florian, Douglas. *Summersaults.* New York: Greenwillow Books, 2002.

Ford, Carolyn. *Nothing in the Mailbox.* Katonah, NY: Richard C. Owen Publishers, Inc., 1996.

George, Kristine O'Connell. *Old Elm Speaks: Tree Poems.* New York, Clarion Books, 1998.

Goodman, Susan. *On This Spot: An Expedition Back Through Time.* New York: Greenwillow Books, 2004.

Hassanein, Amany F. *Little Puffer Fish.* Katonah, NY: Richard C. Owen Publishers, Inc., 2000.

Heard, Georgia. *Awakening the Heart.* Portsmouth, NH: Heinemann, 1999.

Heard, Georgia. *For the Good of the Earth and Sun.* Portsmouth, NH: Heinemann, 1989.

Heard, Georgia. *This Place I Know: Poems of Comfort.* Cambridge, MA: Candlewick Press, 2002.

Henkes, Kevin. *Jessica.* New York: Greenwillow Books, 1989.

Henkes, Kevin. *Owen.* New York: Greenwillow Books, 1993.

Hopkins, Lee Bennett. *Lives: Poems About Famous Americans.* New York: HarperCollins Publishers, 1999.

Kasza, Keiko. *Don't Laugh, Joe.* New York: G. P. Putnam's Sons, 1997.

Lunge-Larsen, Lise and Margi Preus. *The Legend of the Lady Slipper.* Boston: Houghton Mifflin Company, 1999.

McPhail, David. *Mole Music.* New York: Henry Holt and Company, 1999.

Munsch, Robert N. *The Paper Bag Princess.* Toronto, Canada: Annick Press, Ltd., 1980.

Peters, Lisa Westberg. *Earthshake: Poems from the Ground Up.* New York: Greenwillow Books, 2003.

Ray, Katie Wood. *What You Know by Heart: How to Develop Curriculum for Your Writing Workshop.* Portsmouth, NH: Heinemann, 2002.

Ray, Katie Wood. *Wondrous Words.* Urbana, IL: National Council of Teachers of English, 1999.

Root, Phyllis. *Oliver Finds His Way.* Cambridge, MA: Candlewick Press, 2002.

Routman, Regie. *Conversations.* Portsmouth, NH: Heinemann, 2000.

Routman, Regie. *Kid's Poems: Teaching Second Graders to Love Writing Poetry.* New York: Scholastic, 2000.

Routman, Regie. *Kid's Poems: Teaching Third and Fourth Graders to Love Writing Poetry.* New York: Scholastic, 2000.

Ryan, Pam Munoz. *When Marian Sang: True Recital of Marian Anderson.* New York: Scholastic, 2002.

St. George, Judith. *So You Want to Be President?* New York: Philomel, 2000.

Schaefer, Lola M. *Baron: Rescue Dog.* Katonah, NY: Richard C. Owen Publishers, Inc., 2000.

Schaefer, Lola M. *Pick, Pull, Snap! Where Once a Flower Bloomed.* New York: Greenwillow Books, 2003.

Schertle, Alice. *A Lucky Thing.* San Diego: Harcourt Brace and Co., 1997.

Shahan, Sherry. *The Hungry Sea Star.* Katonah, NY: Richard C. Owen Publishers, Inc., 1997.

Shannon, George. *Tippy-Toe Chick, Go!* New York: Greenwillow Books, 2003.

Singer, Marilyn. *Fireflies at Midnight.* New York: Atheneum Books for Young Readers, 2003.

Worth, Valerie. *all the small poems.* New York: Farrar, Straus and Giroux, 1987.